Parents are often surprised by the quality and the depth of their child's memory and observation, and many are beginning to recognise that the best time to learn is when everything is new and therefore important to the child.

Here is a series of six books designed to help parents to amuse, interest and at the same time to teach. *Shapes, Colours* and the Ladybird *abc* each have their part to play in bringing the child to an early understanding of the reading process; *Counting* teaches him to recognise and understand simple numbers, and *Telling the Time* shows him how to relate the time on a clock face to his everyday life. *Big and Little* deals with the words which describe relative sizes and positions, all shown through objects and scenes which will be familiar to the young child.

© LADYBIRD BOOKS LTD MCMLXXVIII

shapes

by ETHEL WINGFIELD

designed by HARRY WINGFIELD

illustrated by JOHN SCOTT and HARRY WINGFIELD

Ladybird Books Loughborough

Everything around us
has a **shape**.

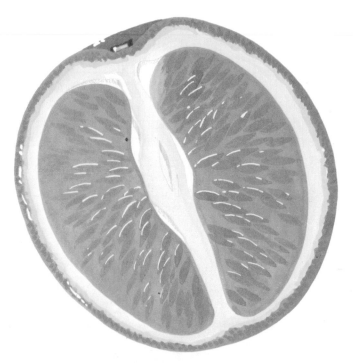

This orange
has a shape.

Its shape is called
a **circle**.

A **circle** shape.

Circle means
round,
very round . . .

. . . no corners

. . . it can roll.

You can see
circles everywhere.

If you could squash down
a circle
you would get an **oval**.

This egg's shape
is called **oval.**

Ovals can be **fat** or **thin.**

Look for **oval** shapes in fruit and flowers.

This shape is called
a **square**.

It has **4** sides
all the same

and **4** corners
all the same.

How many **squares** ?

This boy
has **squares** on his shirt.

A **rectangle** has a shap

2 **long** sides

ike a square

... only longer.

and 2 **short** sides.

How many **rectangles** can you see?

quares all round the house.

These shapes are all called **triangles**.

Each one has **3** sides and **3** corners.

How many **triangles** can you see ?

Letters are shapes.

So are the kind
you post !

Numbers are shapes.

0 1 2 3 4

These are shells.

Some things don't have
special shape names.

What do you think these shapes are?

Find another like this

and this

and this

Do you know what these signs mean ?

You can cut up shapes into other shapes.

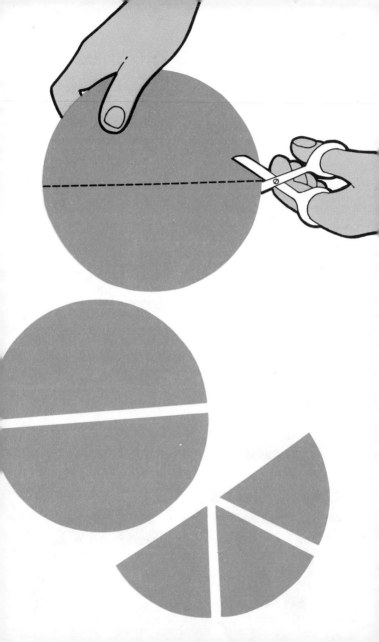

You can make pictures
with shapes.

Draw some shapes.

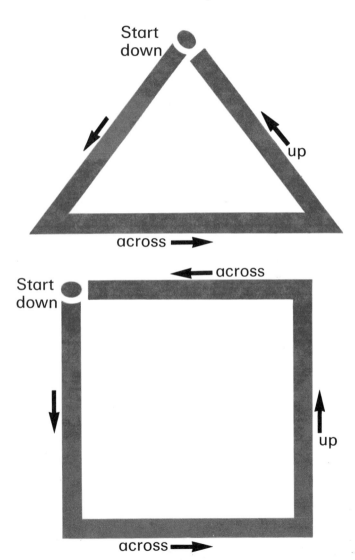